Why Do We Have Seasons?

WHY IS IT Summer?

Sara L. Latta

Enslow Elementary

an imprint of

Enslow Publishers, Inc.

40 Industrial Road
Box 398
Berkeley Heights, NJ 07922
USA

http://www.enslow.com

Words to Know

pollen (PAHL ehn)—Tiny grains made by flowers that allow seeds to grow into new plants.

Yellow pollen is on this flower.

tilt (TIHLT)—To tip to one side. Earth tilts as it goes around the sun.

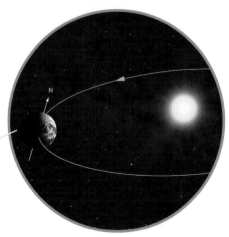

Earth is tilted.

Contents

What are the seasons?

Winter, spring, summer, fall—these are the four seasons of the year.

fall

winter

spring

Each season lasts about three months. The seasons change from cold to warm, then back to cold. Summer is the warmest season.

Summer

When is it summer?

The earth goes around the sun one time each year. Earth tilts as it goes around the sun.

North Pole

Summer

Winter

When the North Pole tilts toward the sun, the north part of Earth has summer.

Earth's path
around sun

The first day of summer in
North America is around June 21.

Winter

Summer

South Pole

When the South Pole
tilts toward the sun,
the south part of
Earth has summer.

How Does Earth's tilt make summer weather warm?

Let's look at summer in the north part of Earth. The north part of Earth tilts toward the sun in summer. The sun's rays fall straight on this part of Earth. This makes summer sunlight very strong.

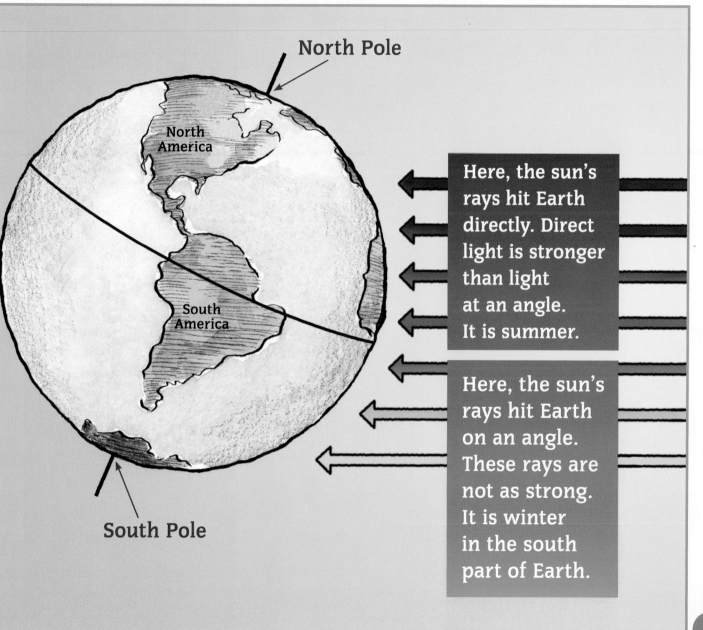

North Pole

North America

South America

Here, the sun's rays hit Earth directly. Direct light is stronger than light at an angle. It is summer.

Here, the sun's rays hit Earth on an angle. These rays are not as strong. It is winter in the south part of Earth.

South Pole

What else makes summer warm?

Summer days have more hours of sunlight than winter days. There is more time to warm the air, water, and land.

The summer heat also causes rain, wind, lightning, and thunder.

How Do Summer Days help Plants grow?

Plants use sunlight to make food. Plants get water from summer rains. This food and water helps plants grow. From the short grass to tall trees, many plants grow fast in summer.

Many plants have colorful flowers in the summer. Bees and butterflies spread pollen from plant to plant. Then the plant can make seeds. The seeds will make new plants.

pollen

13

What Do animals Do in the summer?

chipmunk

Leafy trees and bushes make good homes for birds and other animals. There is plenty of food for the animals to eat. Young animals grow and learn about their world in the summer.

white-tailed deer

opossums

15

What Do Farmers Do in the Summer?

Summer is a busy time for farmers. The summer sunlight makes crops grow fast. Farmers grow wheat for our bread. They grow juicy peaches and crunchy carrots for us to eat.

What Do Children Do in the Summer?

Most schools have a summer break. This is a good time to go on a trip. Many people go swimming, hiking, or camping. What do you like to do on long summer days?

Do Plants need sunlight to grow?

You will need:

- ☀ potting soil
- ☀ 4 small paper cups
- ☀ sunflower seeds or bean seeds
- ☀ water
- ☀ plastic wrap

1. Put some potting soil into four small paper cups.

2. Press two or three seeds into the soil in each cup.

3. Pour some water into each cup.

4. Cover each cup with plastic wrap. Put the cups in a sunny spot. Check your pots every day. Don't let them dry out!

5. When the seeds start to sprout, remove the plastic wrap. Put two of the containers in a shady place. Leave the other two in the sunny spot. Which plants grow better? Why? As your plants grow, move them to a larger pot.

Learn More

Books

Branley, Franklyn, M. *Sunshine Makes the Seasons*. New York: HarperCollins Publishers, 2005.

Blexbolex. *Seasons.* New York: Enchanted Lions Books, 2010.

McClure, Nikki. *Mamma, Is It Summer Yet?* New York: Abrams Books for Young Readers, 2010.

McKneally, Ranida T. and Grace Lin. *Our Seasons.* Massachusetts: Perfection Learning, 2007.

Web Sites

Earth and Atmospheric Science fun at NCAR "Kids Crossing".
<http://www.eo.ucar.edu/kids/index.html>
This is a great site for science education.

"Apples for the teacher"
<http://www.apples4theteacher.com/holidays/summer/first-day-of-summer.html>
Use this web site to find fun summer crafts, games and activities.

The Weather channel offers "the weather channel kids".
<http://www.theweatherchannelkids.com>
This site offers interactive "weather fun" for kids.

Index

Enslow Elementary, an imprint of Enslow Publishers, Inc.

Enslow Elementary® is a registered trademark of Enslow Publishers, Inc.

Copyright © 2012 by Enslow Publishers, Inc.

All rights reserved.

No part of this book may be reproduced by any means without the written permission of the publisher.

Original edition published as *What Happens in Summer* in 1996.

Library of Congress Cataloging-in-Publication Data

Latta, Sara L.

    Why is it summer? / Sara L. Latta.
       p. cm. – (Why do we have seasons?)
    Summary: "Read about when summer begins, why do we have seasons, how do summer days help plants grow, and what farmers do in the summer"–Provided by publisher.
    Previous ed.: What happens in summer? / Sara L. Latta. ©2006.
    Includes bibliographical references and index.
    ISBN 978-0-7660-3987-2
    I. Latta, Sara L. What happens in summer? II. Title.
    QB637.6.L38 2012
    508.2–dc23   2011019307

Paperback ISBN 978-1-59845-390-4
ePUB ISBN 978-1-4645-0438-9
PDF ISBN 978-1-4646-0483-6

Printed in the United States of America.

022013 Lake Book Manufacturing, Inc., Melrose Park, IL

10 9 8 7 6 5 4 3 2

To Our Readers: We have done our best to make sure all Internet addresses in this book were active and appropriate when we went to press. However, the author and the publisher have no control over and assume no liability for the material available on those Internet sites or on other Web sites they may link to. Any comments or suggestions can be sent by e-mail to comments@enslow.com or to the address on the back cover.

♻ Enslow Publishers, Inc., is committed to printing our books on recycled paper. The paper in every book contains 10% to 30% post-consumer waste (PCW). The cover board on the outside of each book contains 100% PCW. Our goal is to do our part to help young people and the environment too!

Note to Parents and Teachers: The **Why Do We Have Seasons?** series supports the National Science Education Standards for K–4 science. The Words to Know section introduces subject-specific vocabulary words, including pronunciation and definitions. Early readers may need help with these new words.

Photo Credits: © Corel Corporation, pp. 4–5, 20–23; © 2005 Jupiter Images Corporation, pp. 20–21; Mark Garlick/Photo Researchers, pp. 6–7; © 2011 Photos.com, a division of Getty Images. All rights reserved, pp. 2, 8, 10–19; Tom Labaff, p. 9.

Cover Photo: ©2011 Photos.Com, a division of Getty Images. All rights reserved.

Science Consultant, Harold Brooks, PhD, NOAA/National Severe Storms Laboratory, Norman, Oklahoma

Series Literacy Consultant, Allan A. De Fina, PhD,
Dean, College of Education/Professor of Literacy Education
New Jersey City University
Past President of the New Jersey Reading Association